HILARY DUFF

ACTRESS AND SINGER

by
Marylou Morano Kjelle

P.O. Box 196
Hockessin, Delaware 19707
Visit us on the web: www.mitchelllane.com
Comments? email us: mitchelllane@mitchelllane.com

Printing   1   2   3   4   5   6   7   8   9

A Robbie Reader

Hilary Duff	Thomas Edison	Albert Einstein
Philo T. Farnsworth	Henry Ford	Robert Goddard
Mia Hamm	Tony Hawk	LeBron James
Donovan McNabb	Dr. Seuss	Charles Schulz

Library of Congress Cataloging-in-Publication Data
Kjelle, Marylou Morano
       Hilary Duff / by Marylou Morano Kjelle.
           p. cm. — (A Robbie reader)
   Discography: p.
   Filmography: p.
   Includes bibliographical references and index.
     ISBN 1-58415-295-8 (library bound)
   1. Duff, Hilary, 1987- 2. Actors—United States—Biography—Juvenile literature. I. Title.
II. Series.
PN2287.D79K58 2005
792.02'8'092--dc22
                                     2004009303

ABOUT THE AUTHOR: Marylou Morano Kjelle is a freelance writer and photojournalist who lives and works in central New Jersey. She is a regular contributor to several local newspaper and online publications. Marylou writes a column for the *Westfield Leader/Times of Scotch Plains--Fanwood* called "Children's Book Nook," where she reviews children's books. She has written eight nonfiction books for young readers and has an M.S. degree in Science from Rutgers University.

PHOTO CREDITS: Cover: Kevin Winter/Getty Images; p. 4 Frederick M. Brown/Getty Images; p. 6 Mike Guastella/WireImage.com; p. 8, top, Giulio Marcocchi/Getty Images; bottom, Albert L. Ortega/WireImage.com; p. 10 Peter Kramer/Getty Images; p. 12 Steve Granitz/WireImage.com; p. 14 Robert Mora/Getty Images; p. 16, top, Lester Cohen/WireImage.com; bottom, Jim Spellman/WireImage.com; p.18 David Sprague/WireImage.com; p. 19 Globe Photos, Inc.; p. 20 Lee Celano/WireImage.com; p. 22 Mike Guastella/WireImage.com; p. 24, top, Michel Porro/Getty Images; bottom, Tim Mosenfelder/Getty Images; p 26 Frank Micelotta/Getty Images; p. 27 Ray Amati/Getty Images

ACKNOWLEDGMENTS: The following story has been thoroughly researched, and to the best of our knowledge, represents a true story. While every possible effort has been made to ensure accuracy, the publisher will not assume liability for damages caused by inaccuracies in the data, and makes no warranty on the accuracy of the information contained herein. This story has not been authorized nor endorsed by Hilary Duff.

TABLE OF CONTENTS

Here is Hilary at the Nickelodeon Kid's Choice Awards. Since she began starring in *Lizzie McGuire*, she is invited to attend many popular events.

MEET LIZZIE McGUIRE

In the spring of 2000, the Disney Channel was planning a new television show. It was called *What's Lizzie Thinking?* The show would be about a schoolgirl named Lizzie. To reveal what Lizzie was thinking, the scenes (seenz) would switch from **live action** to a spunky, animated (AH-nuh-MAY-ted) cartoon of the girl.

A special person was needed to play Lizzie. Lizzie was a normal teenager who did regular things. The girl who was going to play Lizzie had to be a normal teenager, too. Many girls wanted to be Lizzie. Only one was right for the part. That girl was Hilary Duff. She was thirteen years old.

CHAPTER ONE

Hilary enjoys spending time with her friends both on and off the set.

The name of the show was changed to *Lizzie McGuire.* It aired on TV for the first time on January 19, 2001. *Lizzie McGuire* and its star, Hilary Duff, were big hits. Hilary had been a ballet (bal-AY) dancer. She had acted in movies. But she had never been in a television show before. Now she was a new star.

Hilary poses with her father, Bob, and her mother, Susan.

Hilary and her sister, Haylie, are very close. They go lots of places together.

"HIL"

Hilary Ann Duff was born on September 28, 1987, in Houston (HYOOS-tin), Texas. Her family calls her Hil. Hilary's mother is Susan Duff. She travels with Hilary and helps with her career (cah-REER). Her father is Bob Duff. He owns **convenience** (con-VEEN-yence) **stores**. Hilary has one sister named Haylie. Haylie is two years older than Hilary. She is an actress, too.

When they were children, Hilary adored (uh-DOORD) her big sister. Whatever Haylie did, Hilary wanted to do, too. Haylie took ballet lessons, so Hilary took ballet lessons. Hilary was a good dancer. When she was six years old, Hilary danced in *The Nutcracker*.

Since moving to California with her mother and sister, Hilary has become very famous with her acting and singing. Here she is at a Christmas concert in New York City.

Haylie took acting lessons. Hilary told her mother, "Mom, I want to do that." Hilary took acting lessons with Haylie. When Hilary was seven years old, she was in her first commercial (com-ER-shuhl). Soon after, she had a small part in a television **miniseries** (min-ee-SEER-ees) called *True Women.* Haylie also had a small part in the show.

Both Duff sisters wanted to be actors. They asked their parents to take them to California. There they would have more **opportunities** to work in movies and on television. In 1996, Hilary, Haylie, and Susan moved to Los Angeles (loss ANJ-el-iss). Bob stayed in Houston to run his stores.

Hilary gives the camera a big "thumbs-up." Being a famous actress, Hilary is used to posing for many pictures.

A MOVE TO CALIFORNIA

In California, Susan searched for work for Hilary and Haylie. Acting jobs were not easy to find. Hilary tried out for many parts. She was never hired. Finally, in 1997, Hilary got the part of Wendy, the witch in the movie *Casper Meets Wendy.* Hilary acted so well that she was **nominated** for a Young Actress Award. She didn't win the award. Still, it made her happy to know that people thought she was a good actor.

Hilary kept busy with TV work. She made a TV movie called *The Soul Collector.* She appeared on a TV show called *Chicago Hope.* By 2001, Hilary was starring in *Lizzie McGuire.* She worked long hours on the set playing

At the 16th Annual Kids' Choice Awards, Hilary and two cast members of *Lizzie McGuire*, Jake Thomas and Adam Lamberg, accept the award for Favorite TV Show.

Lizzie. A set is the place where the taping (TAY-ping) of a show or movie takes place. Hilary also had schoolwork to do. A teacher came to the set to help her with her schooling. Hilary studied between takes, or the times she was acting. First she would work. Then she would study. "I keep going back and forth all day," Hilary said at the time.

In all, Hilary made sixty-five *Lizzie McGuire* episodes. The show made her famous. Wherever she went, people knew her. They asked for her **autograph** or to take her picture. In 2003, *Lizzie McGuire* won a Nickelodeon Kids' Choice Award for Favorite TV Show.

The people at the Disney Channel were happy with *Lizzie McGuire.* In 2002, they asked Hilary to star in a TV movie called *Cadet Kelly.* The movie made TV history. The first night it aired, more people watched it than the **premiere** of any other original (or-IJ-IN-al) Disney TV movie.

This is the cast of *The Lizzie McGuire Movie*. Hilary is in the second row.

Hilary smiles as she signs autographs for her fans.

MORE MOVIES FOR HILARY

Hilary's success with *Lizzie McGuire* and *Cadet Kelly* led to more movie roles. Three movies starring Hilary were released in 2003. First came *Agent Cody Banks,* a teenage action spy film. Hilary plays Natalie Connors, a scientist's daughter. Cody is played by Frankie Muniz (MYOO-nez). Cody and Natalie fall in love in the movie.

The Lizzie McGuire Movie came next. The movie shows Lizzie in high school. Hilary plays two parts. She is Lizzie and an Italian singer named Isabella. Part of the movie was filmed in Rome, Italy. "I ate pizza twice a day every day," Hilary said.

Hilary and Frankie Muniz star together in *Agent Cody Banks*. Here Hilary and Frankie pose together.

In another 2003 movie, Hilary plays Lorraine (low-RAIN) in *Cheaper by the Dozen*. This movie is the true story of a family with twelve children. The story "shows the struggles of parents dealing with a family," Hilary said.

She also acted in a movie that was co-produced by her mother, Susan Duff. Called *A Cinderella Story,* it is a new take on the Cinderella fairy tale. Hilary plans to work on many more movies in the future.

Hilary enjoys acting in movies. This photo of Hilary and co-star Steve Martin was taken during a scene of *Cheaper by the Dozen*.

Just like a normal teenager, Hilary has two pet dogs that she loves to play with.

A NORMAL KID

Although Hilary is famous, she sees herself as a normal teenager. At home, Hilary does chores. She loves animals and has two pet dogs. She does schoolwork. She likes math and world history. She wants to go to college one day.

Hilary's family is important to her. They help her choose good acting roles. Hilary wants young people to enjoy her movies and television programs.

Hilary enjoys watching movies herself. Two of her favorite stars are Jennifer Lopez and Kate Hudson. She also likes to dance and listen to music. Britney Spears, Vanessa (vuh-NESS-uh) Carlton, and Michelle Branch are some of her favorite singers.

Hilary enjoys being part of charity events. Here she is with her sister and a friend, hosting a charity event for Kids with a Cause.

Hilary and her friends go swimming. They also shop at the mall. Hilary also goes on dates. She likes boys who are smart.

At times it is hard for Hilary to do regular things like eat in a restaurant. Her fans are everywhere. She knows how much they love her and is always nice to them. "They're the people who let me do what I love to do everyday . . . it's so much easier to be nice to them than to be rude," she said.

Hilary likes to **volunteer**. One of her favorite charities is Kids with a Cause. It helps poor and sick children. Hilary would like more young people to volunteer to help the needy.

Besides acting, Hilary also loves singing.

Hilary and her sister Haylie sing together on stage.

A BRIGHT FUTURE

Hilary has other talents besides acting. She likes to sing. Her songs are on the soundtracks of *Lizzie McGuire, The Lizzie McGuire Movie,* and *The Santa Clause 2.*

Hilary has recorded several CDs. Her first was *Santa Claus Lane.* It is an album of Christmas songs. In 2003, Hilary released *Metamorphosis.* Hilary's sister, Haylie, wrote some of the songs on the CD. One song, "So Yesterday," was a hit single. Hilary says her music is a mix of pop and rock, but more rock.

Hilary loves clothes and make-up. She says, "I'm the kind of person who doesn't like to wear things over and over again." She

Hilary poses with her award at Nickelodeon's 17th Annual Kids' Choice Awards. Hilary enjoys **receiving** (ree-CEE-ving) awards because she knows that she worked hard for them.

created her own line of clothing called "Stuff by Duff." She is also working on a line of makeup.

She looks forward to acting in more movies and TV shows. Between acting, singing, designing her own items, and being a normal teenager, Hilary is a very busy girl—a busy girl with a bright future.

Hilary is always volunteering to help people. Here she is hosting the Read to **Achieve** (ah-CHEEV) Celebration.

1987 Hilary Ann Duff is born on September 28.

1996 Hilary, her mother, Susan, and her sister, Haylie, move to California.

1997 Hilary gets the part of Wendy in *Casper and Wendy.*

1998 Hilary is nominated for a Young Actress Award.

2000 Hilary lands the part of Lizzie in Disney Channel's series *Lizzie McGuire.*

2002 Hilary stars in *Cadet Kelly.* On the first night it airs, it makes TV history.

2003 *Lizzie McGuire* wins the Nickelodeon Kids' Choice Award for Favorite TV Show. Three movies starring Hilary Duff are released. They are *Agent Cody Banks, The Lizzie McGuire Movie,* and *Cheaper by the Dozen.* Hilary releases her second solo music CD, *Metamorphosis.*

2004 Hilary launches her own line of clothing, cosmetics, and jewelry. *A Cinderella Story* is released.

FILMOGRAPHY AND DISCOGRAPHY

Filmography

2004 *A Cinderella Story*
2003 *Cheaper by the Dozen*
     The Lizzie McGuire Movie
     Agent Cody Banks
2002 *Cadet Kelly* (TV)
2001 *Human Nature*
1999 *The Soul Collector* (TV)
1998 *Casper Meets Wendy*
1997 *True Women* (TV Movie)–(Hilary did not receive credit
     for appearing in this film)

Discography

2003 *Metamorphosis*
     The Lizzie McGuire Movie (Soundtrack)
        "Why Not?"
        "What Dreams are Made Of"
        "Why Not (McMix)"
2002 *The Santa Clause 2* (Soundtrack)
        "Santa Claus Lane"
     Santa Claus Lane (Christmas album)
     Disneymania (Various artists)
        "The Tiki, Tiki, Tiki Room"
     Lizzie McGuire (Soundtrack)
        "I Can't Wait"

FIND OUT MORE

Books

Boone, Mary. *Hilary Duff: Total Hilary, Metamorphosis, Lizzie McGuire and More.* Chicago: Triumph Books, 2003.

Dower, Laura. *Hanging With Hilary Duff.* Danbury, Conn.: Scholastic, 2003.

Krulik, Nancy. *Hilary Duff: A Not So Typical Teen.* New York: Simon Spotlight, 2003.

Web Addresses

Hilary Duff Central: http://hilaryduffcentral.com

Hilary Duff Official Fan Site: http://www.hilaryduff.com

Hilary Online: http://www.hilaryonline.tk/

The *Lizzie McGuire Movie* Web Site: http://disney.go.com/disneypictures/lizzie/

autograph (AW-tuh-graff)—to sign a name

convenience (con-VEEN-yence) store—a small store that is easy to get to

live action—showing real people in motion, instead of drawn as cartoons or using photographs

miniseries (mih-nee-SEE-rees)—a television movie shown in parts over several days

nominated (NAH-mih-NAY-ted)—named for a prize or political office

opportunities (ah-pur-TOO-nih-tees)—chances

premiere (preh-MEER)—the first time something is shown to the public

volunteer (vah-lun-TEER)—to help someone willingly or to do something without pay